SandCastle

Word Families Set 1

-ap as in cap

Mary Elizabeth Salzmann

Consulting Editor Monica Marx, M.A./Reading Specialist

ABDO
Publishing Company

Published by SandCastle™, an imprint of ABDO Publishing Company, 4940 Viking Drive, Edina, Minnesota 55435.

Printed in the United States.

Credits
Edited by: Pam Price
Curriculum Coordinator: Nancy Tuminelly
Cover and Interior Design and Production: Mighty Media
Photo Credits: Corbis Images, Creatas, Digital Vision, Kelly Doudna, Eyewire Images, Hemera, PhotoDisc, Stockbyte

Library of Congress Cataloging-in-Publication Data

Salzmann, Mary Elizabeth, 1968-
　　-Ap as in cap / Mary Elizabeth Salzmann.
　　　　p. cm. -- (Word families. Set I)
　　Summary: Introduces, in brief text and illustrations, the use of the letter combination "ap" in such words as "cap," "trap," "map," and "wrap."
　　ISBN 1-59197-224-8
　　1. Readers (Primary) [1. Vocabulary. 2. Reading.] I. Title.

PE1119 .S2342146 2003
428.1--dc21
2002038623

SandCastle™ books are created by a professional team of educators, reading specialists, and content developers around five essential components that include phonemic awareness, phonics, vocabulary, text comprehension, and fluency. All books are written, reviewed, and leveled for guided reading, early intervention reading, and Accelerated Reader® programs and designed for use in shared, guided, and independent reading and writing activities to support a balanced approach to literacy instruction.

Let Us Know

After reading the book, SandCastle would like you to tell us your stories about reading. What is your favorite page? Was there something hard that you needed help with? Share the ups and downs of learning to read. We want to hear from you! To get posted on the ABDO Publishing Company Web site, send us e-mail at:

sandcastle@abdopub.com

SandCastle Level: Transitional

-ap Words

cap

clap

lap

map

strap

trap

Lisa is wearing a blue
baseball cap.

Tina and Holly clap
their hands together.

Gabe holds his dog in his lap.

Five kids color a big map.

Gail's bag has a
shoulder strap.

Ben is caught in his
friends' trap.

Zap and
the Chap

Once there was a chap
who wore a scarf and cap.

One day
he went for a walk
and followed a map.

The chap saw a track
and ran a lap.

He passed some trees
that were dripping sap.

He came to a fence
and went through a gap.

The chap found a
stray dog that barked Yap!
He named her Zap.

Suddenly there was lightning and a loud thunder clap.

Zap and the chap
ran home in a snap.

The chap fed Zap kibble
and a leftover wrap.

He gave Zap
a bowl of fresh water
from the tap.

Zap lay down
in the chap's lap.

And then Zap and the chap
took a long nap.

The -ap Word Family

cap	rap
chap	sap
clap	snap
flap	strap
gap	tap
lap	trap
map	wrap
nap	zap

Glossary

Some of the words in this list may have more than one meaning. The meaning listed here reflects the way the word is used in the book.

kibble dry dog or cat food

lap the area on top of your legs when you are sitting down; one time around a track or across a swimming pool and back

sap liquid that is inside trees and plants; sap from maple trees is made into syrup

tap a device that controls the flow of water or other liquid, like a sink faucet

trap something that is used to capture an animal

About SandCastle™

A professional team of educators, reading specialists, and content developers created the SandCastle™ series to support young readers as they develop reading skills and strategies and increase their general knowledge. The SandCastle™ series has four levels that correspond to early literacy development in young children. The levels are provided to help teachers and parents select the appropriate books for young readers.

Emerging Readers
(no flags)

Beginning Readers
(1 flag)

Transitional Readers
(2 flags)

Fluent Readers
(3 flags)

These levels are meant only as a guide. All levels are subject to change.

To see a complete list of SandCastle™ books and other nonfiction titles from ABDO Publishing Company, visit www.abdopub.com or contact us at:

4940 Viking Drive, Edina, Minnesota 55435 • 1-800-800-1312 • fax: 1-952-831-1632